I0840943

TOAD TO PRINCE

Karen Kellock Ph.D.

Manual for
Superior Men

A complete theory based on Einstein physics, Political Psychology, Systems Theory and Archetypal Psychiatry.

FORMULA

**All success attraction
All disease obstruction
All recovery elimination**

You must fast on all three

OBSTRUCTIONS:

**People
Habit
Food**

TOAD TO PRINCE

Don't envy when the enemy flourishes like a green tree for just as suddenly he's mowed down, trust me. The wicked hang together like peas in a pod but you're fortified by God.   They come from good stock in looks but degenerate quickly thru sin: has-beens.   When God pulls the plug on beauty it's a sudden thing--all light turns muddy-- but He restores youth as the eagle so it's not irrevocable.

FALLEN SOCIETY

MEAN GIRLS NOW RULE
MAGNET TO MAGGOTS
THEY'RE CHEAP, YOU'RE NOT
THEY WANNA MOVE IN
TAKE A YEAR TO FIND SELF
NEVER LET EM MOVE IN!
ADVICE: DON'T LET EM IN AT ALL
WE MAL-ADAPT TO GUESTS
AREN'T YOU BEING USED?
THEY WERE ALWAYS JEALOUS
AREN'T YOU WASTING TIME?
PEOPLE COME AND GO
IT'S A FALLEN SOCIETY
THE ANTI-FEMALE SPIRIT
IT'S ALL ABOUT PEOPLE
WE ARE BIOCOMPUTERS
CHAMPIONS ARE ALONE
THEY HATE YOU FOR GOD'S BLESSINGS
MEN WANT SEX—SO WHAT?
MEN TEST RESPONSE
TRUST TAKES TIME
THEY PRESSURE FOR SEX
CHOCOLATE AND SELF-CONTROL

FALLEN SOCIETY

Fornication culture ruined the family. Cohabitation & abortion has completely changed society.

God said: "Your suffering was your work, part two was writing about it and now you're in retirement".

When you wake up you see you were plotted against the whole time. It took me 30 years to see it, aye.

You weren't supposed to make it outa the situation but you were prepared and now they're wonderin'

They set a trap and you stealthfully escaped just as you always did cuz God at the last minute came.

They didn't expect you to not only escape but improve so much while they stay the same, stuck.

They say they're happy for you but they're not. It's so easy to see through them, why not do it.

Don't have blind loyalty to anybody. People and situations change so you don't know see.

MEAN GIRLS NOW RULE

Mean girls like "The View" love the joy of rejecting an outsider, knowing nothing but they hate her.

They can't have their lame assumptions challenged. That's why the anger or running backwards.

When they discard you it's a class thing. They loved you at first but then viewed you as the dregs see.

Cucks, clowns, Jezebels, the stupid, the horrendous, reptilian consciousness: today's madness.

FALLEN SOCIETY

Your face shows structure, solidity and divinity cuz you no longer worship people and their insanity.

MAGNET TO MAGGOTS

If a courting man's not offering you something he's coming to take something: forget him honey.

He's in it for the take, not to give and that's not gonna change, so leave. It's TAKE or GIVE.

He pushes to move in, but he's not offering to help you any he's just wanting to help himself honey.

You lost his respect when you let him move in. This is YOUR house where you're in charge friend.

Does he brings his laundry over? When there's a laundromat down the street there? Beware.

Men always wanna move in with me. I spend money on neat things & my home is a happy sanctuary.

THEY'RE CHEAP, YOU'RE NOT

They're too cheap to spend on neat things so they come to you darling and you think "I'm starring".

"Smoking good herb teaches you boundaries better than none other cuz they ALL wanna come over". Lady

They wanna come over so bad I fear violence if I refuse so I say "my family is here, sorry no chance."

Losers don't have a life nor the imagination to create one but you do so you're like a magnet too.

You spend money on cigars, exotic sausages and cheeses, liquors: of course they come over.

FALLEN SOCIETY

Women are used. They must learn to stand against it along with what is theirs or they will lose.

THEY WANNA MOVE IN

They wanna move in Paula, you're momma! You keep things neat for the immature men of America.

You only move in with a man when fully committed and paying. Not the other way around darling.

It's too dam easy for you to say "sure, I'll do your laundry" and to feel so loving/altruistic see.

Get rid of freeloading nobodies. They always love bomb to edge into your world but destroy you sis.

You have to know your value, your own worth. If you don't [or if you buy their bull] you're cursed.

All my dad ever said: "hold your head up high" cuz the herd's always trying to break you down, aye.

You gotta be ready for it and you can't trust anyone. Be loyal to yourself now and don't give a dam.

TAKE A YEAR TO FIND SELF

Take a year off to find your true self: be celibate. You'll be so gloriously unique you win all bets.

Men have broken you down til you're just an ordinary blob serving appetitive needs day in/out.

Sex brings exchange of spirits. His dullness is now inhabited in you as you proceed to lowness.

Take a year to find who you really are: what makes you happy and what you desire from life truly.

FALLEN SOCIETY

By staying celibate you harness that most powerful sexual energy, to later manifest it ALL see.

NEVER LET EM MOVE IN!

Women, to stay the beautiful, loving ace: Don't ever allow these men to move into your place.

We are homemakers, **NESTERS**. Of course they wanna live here but they gotta commit and pay first.

I can't let a man in my home cuz he won't want to leave. The contrast with the world is too great see.

They could just make a home for themselves like we, but they won't/can't cuz it's about maturity.

Women lend a man their car right away, their key to the house, even their credit cards, ouch.

Why do we do these things so reflexively? Because we want a man/were told it's our reason for living.

You're always cooking for him. Does he replace the food? Does he contribute to you fool?

ADVICE: DON'T LET EM IN AT ALL

I got so low it never occurred to me how happy I'd be alone if only my guests would leave NOW.

We degrade self to adapt to unwanted guests. It's a way of going dense when they couldn't care less.

Once you close that door behind them anything can happen. I'm telling you, don't let em in.

Women stupidly think they'll hook a man thru sex but altho' it effects he's lost necessary respect.

FALLEN SOCIETY

They always pretend and promise all they'll do for you once they move in but they never will fool.

Your home is YOUR domain. Only your rich prince charming giving you a ring may remain.

Of course they wanna come in outa the rain and eat up all your gains but this will bring you down again.

If he moves in your home it's still ALL on you--you're responsible for it all, not him you fool.

WE MAL-ADAPT TO GUESTS

We mal-adapt to guests by taking on their thing and leaving ours behind, taking TOO MUCH TIME.

Cuza all these sticky bands around people, relocation was a spring breeze like on vacation too.

They wanna wash their clothes: "go to a laundromat". They wanna borrow money: "go to a bank".

Stay a queen: realize how happy you are alone friend, never lend and never give a minute again.

The greatest luxury in this world is true independence from people, no longer being controlled at all.

We're meek Christians--they see it as weakness--but as a point we're like bears: get outa my house!

AREN'T YOU BEING USED?

Like the singer says, they wanna PIECE of you: what you have and copy your winning personality too.

If they're not into independence--building their own life--they'll try to absorb yours and move in, aye.

FALLEN SOCIETY

They want to hit you up cuz they don't have it: they can't dig like you dig--these people aren't solid.

If you're solid a buncha weaklings try to use you. They can't get what you can get, that's it Sue.

How many times have you done favors for somebody and they turned out to be the enemy?

THEY WERE ALWAYS JEALOUS

They were always jealous of you and they're your enemies now cuz you're so successful.

They were never with you friend and when they get their own stuff you'll never hear from em again.

It doesn't have to be money, sex or food. They use for emotional support/free therapy/texting buddy.

Some people email or text you constantly. Then it all drops off: you were used for that time see.

It's not that we're stingy or selfish. We just can't allow ourselves to be used, this should be obvious.

I may sound rough but you gotta be this way in this latter day cuza all this BS coming our way.

You'll never get that time back you gave to one you thought was a keeper: gotta be more clever.

It's so stupid to be used by people who aren't even with you. But we do it all the time to be approved.

AREN'T YOU WASTING TIME?

It's a waste of time cuz they gain more from you then you gain yourself while ur pulled down too.

FALLEN SOCIETY

You don't just keep buying and giving. The next time they gotta buy but that they're not seeing.

People have to be on a similar wavelength. They gotta do things you can do & have similar strengths.

They'd never yoke a horse and donkey together as one is held down. Similarly, don't have em around.

When I was filled with friends I literally had none. A boatload of good times then they're gone.

People going against you is a huge motivator. See it as building career muscle as you shoot past her.

And when everyone comes against you it can help you alot: it really gives you the edge after that.

If they haven't been real with you don't give them the time of day and leave em in the dust too.

The man/woman who has overcome all this and gets the gist has structure carved on his face sis.

PEOPLE COME AND GO

People change with time so these emotional attachments will be irrelevant soon, aye.

He's not the same person you grew up with. You don't know what type of energy he has now twit.

Don't let people back & forth outa your life when they've already proven their your enemy, aye!

People will do you so dirty then act like it's nothing or come back like they never did anything.

You wouldn't have these awful feelings today unless they did you dirty but said "oh, it's all ok".

FALLEN SOCIETY

All from jealousy Sue: It's crazy what your haters will do and it's crazy to find out who they are too.

Look what they did to Jesus, the Son of God. They tore him apart--all they did to you is call you odd.

IT'S A FALLEN SOCIETY

Satan is everywhere in a falling society in the gutter. You gotta be ready: dig in and do not fear.

Loyalty surprises me but not backstabbing. I've seen too much: it's not goodness I'm expecting.

What do we have but our homes and dear ones? Family, home, country, God not a globalist mob.

Are you going to bow down to their needs cuz they can't make themselves happy? It's unequal see.

They'll never be on your level so why not self-improve to attract those higher not mal-adapt to lower?

Chocolate: medicine or poison? I'm still asking that question cuz it's so delicious I keep wonderin.

They have huge heads and get triggered if you tell them what's right. This is a low point/human blight.

Your sisters expected you to be in the gutter from all the humiliating, filthy, reputation killing slander.

THE ANTI-FEMALE SPIRIT

Is there anyone ruder & more wrong than a woman? No, go on The View and it's a slaughter fomenting.

If women have pretty privilege they don't have to work for it or improve in character--until later.

FALLEN SOCIETY

Angry triggered females show bright smiles on social media while behind the scenes it's trivia.

They lead you to a land that doesn't even exist. Meet a smiley female on social media in real life sis.

Donald Trump: deter, detain and deport. Joe Biden: invite em all in to destroy America of course.

IT'S ALL ABOUT PEOPLE

Stop fighting with demons in people. See Satan's minions & proceed with your day free of evil.

Left to our own we'd succeed, it's just us. But it's social psychology: other people imprint and smudge.

It's PEOPLE who imprint guilt and shame on us when we didn't do anything. It's people who do it see.

People come and go, age/die and perish. Yet they imprint like God, isn't that odd: they are selfish.

First we're traumatized by people then we work it out until mid aged and pure [free of worldly evil].

Around sixty the original trauma is lessened for good. We wanna be a clean slate and not a hood.

WE ARE BIOCOMPUTERS

We are biocomputers and people input their crap into her. It takes a while to export or delete slurs.

They insulted me so much I decided to see it as a game and excellent practice to bash ego as such.

The only things you should be thinking about are God and separation but protection firstly son.

FALLEN SOCIETY

They wanna come and get what you have instead and If a success they'd rather see you dead.

They risk it for the buiscuit. They like you but will risk losing you just to play the game and you know it.

You only move in with a man when fully committed and paying. Not the other way around darling.

Mad at life cuz they couldn't do what you did, stirring up trouble cuz they jealous anyway: be RID.

They mad cuz God opened up a door for you and not them. They don't see His rewards system.

If they were involved in self-improvement or business they wouldn't be so focused on you sis.

It's GET-YOU or get-Trump that is their main focus, not on doing good things or anything else sis.

I make a cozy home and so do you. Of COURSE they wanna hang here but we're too busy Sue.

CHAMPIONS ARE ALONE

You spend 98% of your time working and they spend the same amount envying and targeting.

The champion must learn to be alone just to avoid the blows be they psychic, verbal or for show.

People are cruel just for the hell of it. Everything changed from the good ol' days, they're out of it.

No round table discussions just speaking from a podium. It's just shit shots if we're with em.

I tell em: if you wanna have what I have, do what I did. But they want it all, right now, totally entitled.

FALLEN SOCIETY

The girls hate the boys just for the hell of it, and as the boys conciliate the girls get even worse ok.

They spend all time and energy trying to make you low in life but God punishes officiousness, aye.

When your neighbor lives peacably beside thee, stirring up trouble is a no-no to the Lord see.

I worked 18 hours a day for fifty years and STILL they're jealous as if it was just given not earned.

I don't like parties cuz someone will say something. Insults: what has happened to earthlings?

THEY HATE YOU FOR GOD'S BLESSINGS

The Lord chose to bless me in front of them and it was a rough road--you know what they were thinkin'.

They drove me into isolation at a young age. I was miserable in sorority and happy alone ok.

The world evolves on--the mazeway--as I marched to a different drummer and became strong.

The more different I became the more they reacted when I showed my face. That's it ok.

The herd evolves TOGETHER. They cycle thru their little dramas and narratives through the years.

I couldn't believe what a bitch she'd become after college. Angry, accusing, impossible to manage.

You weren't part of that current, you've become totally unique and able to stand up against nuts.

MEN WANT SEX—SO WHAT?

FALLEN SOCIETY

The narcissist will be everything you want in the beginning, rushing to sex for bonding.

Sex is how he bonds with you and a soul tie is formed after which it's hell on earth for you Sue.

He rushes you to sex, move in or burn bridges. Tell him you're celibate, he sees it as a challenge.

Once he gets to that point tell him you're celibate but he won't care what you say if he wants it.

He just wants what he wants. But you do your research, be diligent and NEVER cave in to sex nuts.

You shouldn't CARE that he wants it. That is none of your business! Tell em that to defend it.

Men want sex--so what? It's none of your affair what another wants so get your boundaries up.

MEN TEST RESPONSE

Men test response. If you're a boundariless wimp--a rudderless ship--his demands gets worse.

But if you nip it in the bud it's very different from what he sees in everyone else drenched in mud.

Men want someone who's REAL. Most women are not real, it's all a fake thing and they get cruel.

Men want a real woman who is nice--just nice would be so nice! But modern women are not, aye.

One reason their not nice: sex sin has consequences and it's been three generations of this.

Have the guts to stand up against prevailing immorality while your sisters become downright slutty.

FALLEN SOCIETY

Men are giving up on women and why wouldn't they. I've given up too, girlfriends can be difficulty.

They are liberals mostly, voting democrat--they believe that crap so how could we relate to that?

Keep people at a distance, don't get too close. Thoroughly check em out, keep door/legs closed.

Queen advice: do your homework, take it slow. Make sure he's past-clean before getting involved.

A queen interviews men, not the other way around. She doesn't jump in bed, she's checking em out.

TRUST TAKES TIME

If they expect you to trust em right off the bat you know it's a NO. Everyone's on probation ya' know.

The human race has fallen as the END approaches so it's all a matter of management/knowledge.

If a man just rolled out of relationship you don't have sexual relations until he's clean/out of it.

All of the negative energy and toxicity of the prior relationship comes right into you, that's it.

One year no sex but just getting to know them, to trusted friendship and THEN relationship.

THEY PRESSURE FOR SEX

No pressuring you into sex or anything else. And if you slip it's not a contract--you can stop/get out.

If you do it that way you'll have a successful relationship not just another fly by night disappointment.

FALLEN SOCIETY

If you jump into the dating pool you'll be a fish out of water. You don't want that, hang in there.

Women, you have goals. So choose a man above em so you become accustomed to success hon'.

Keep your frequency high, walk with the divine, stay clean and have anything you can see.

Don't "go out to find a man". It's better to make a list of wants/demands then pray to God for "him".

Don't "start a conversation". We all gotta match somewhere, just pray and then wait for him.

We all gotta mate we just don't know where he is. Beating the bushes you find him, that's it.

Don't look for men. Don't approach men. YOU are the prize friend, just interview when they come in.

She's fifty--oh my--and feels desperate enough to settle for the rough but I say NOT: wait up.

CHOCOLATE AND SELF-CONTROL

I believe chocolate can be my friend if I have self-control. Just a few licks/tiny piece that's all.

Just as you panic it urinates out. There's other self-protective mechanisms I believe in cacao.

Cacao is the bean replacing caffeinated coffee. It's a neat trick without the acid reflux I get see.

Just as you panic it has a laxative effect. It does that, constantly upgrading the results you get.

If you start to race suddenly see it as temporary cuz it's your friend and you didn't take too many.

TOAD TO PRINCE
BE NOT CONFORMED

TOXIC PEOPLE BUST BOUNDARIES
RELEASED FROM MENTAL PRISON
SOLUTION TO INNER EMPTINESS
IF YOU'RE UP HE'S DOWN: HOMEOSTASIS
FIND THE NONDESCRIPT MAN
DON'T TELL EM ABOUT SUCCESS
SUCCESS BRINGS REJECTION
THE COMPARATIVE MINDSET
WOMEN BRINGING DOWN THEIR HOUSE
LIFE CAN BE HIGH OR LOW/UP TO YOU
THE QUEEN PRESENCE
TO QUEENS IT'S INTOLERABLE
NONNEGOTIABLE STANDARDS: CAN'T GO LOWER
YOUR MINDSET VS. THE WORLD
CHANGE THE QUEEN'S MIND!
NOW HAVE CONFIDENCE & CERTAINTY
JEALOUSY, ENVY, BITTERNESS
ENVY IS HATRED
DON'T IGNORE THE SIGNS
SCAPEGOATS ARE SENSITIVE EMPATHS
SYRUPY SWEET TO YOUR FACE
MALIGNANT CANCER GROWS WITH AGE
TRIANGULATION-STRANGULATION
HALF TRUTHS AND WEB OF LIES
GOD PULLS PLUG ON BEAUTY: PRINCE TO TOAD
SIN BRINGS UGLIFICATION
VISAGE: SINS SHOUTED FROM ROOFTOPS
GOD RESTORES YOUTH AS THE EAGLE
BUT AS FOR YOU...
GOD SAID WHEN YOU FAST [NOT IF]
DAILY FASTARIANISM FOR SUPERIOR MEN
KINGS NEED NUTRIENTS
ROYALTY GETS PRETTY
FAST FOR BREAKTHROUGHS

TOAD TO PRINCE

BE NOT CONFORMED

PSYCH DRUGS ARE THE DREGS
LOOK GOOD, GET POWE
SHORT FASTS ARE A BLAST
STRONG BODY, OVERCOMING MIND
DAILY FASTING IS FUN
GET CLEAR, HAVE CHEER
RELEASE FROM DIETING MADE ME HIGH
LOOK GOOD/BE STRONG
KILLING CHEMICALS
MULTIPLE CHEMICAL SENSITIVITY HELL
JUST STAY HOME
BODY SWEET
GENTILIZE YOUR SPIRIT
CURE THYSELF
GET QUICK AND SLICK
LOOK GOOD WHEN OLD
IBS IS FROM CHEMTRAILS
GET OUT THE LEAD AND TURN HEADS
THIN, PROPRIOCEPTIVE, SECLUDED
HUMANE DAIRY AND GRASS FED COWS
KRAZY KOLLEGE KIDS WRONG DIET
BE PRODUCTIVE: SIT AND THINK
CREAMY LACTOFRUITARIAN SMOOTHIES
REPRESSED EMOTIONS & FOOD
OUT IN THE COUNTRY BUT STILL SICKLY
BUMP IN THE BELT CUZ NO FRUIT
VIOLENT VEGANS
MODERATION OR MUKBANGS?
OLD LADY DIET IS AN ATTITUDE
HOLLYWOOD CAN'T EVEN IDENTIFY CORRUPTION
TASTE TRIP WHILE STAYING HIGH
LACTOFRUITARIAN DELIGHT
SIMMER ALL DAY
CARNIVORE CURED

TOAD TO PRINCE

Be not conformed to this world but be transformed by the renewal of YOUR mind. Romans 12: 2

Psychologist, proverb author and prolific writer about how crazy people are.

TOXIC PEOPLE BUST BOUNDARIES

Toxic people don't have boundaries/don't respect yours and will trample em down like trash for sure.

Because you were imposed on so much you're ultra self-protected now and embedded high above.

Because you sinned so much & finally repented in disgust there's refinement to you as such.

Toxic sisters are sly, secretive mistresses of manipulation and they really enjoy this thing.

They're not just controlling, they're on a power trip filling em with excitement and adrenalin.

All you can do is isolate from the savages. With wisdom turn the ship around em a couple notches.

RELEASED FROM MENTAL PRISON

Imagine you were in a prison then released. Now you're in a mansion and crying over the past?

Stop going through your horrendous lessons. You had to have them so that now you're the don.

TOAD TO PRINCE

Because you wasted years with bad company and finally got away, not you're with a good guy ok.

She was so immature she'd probably have chosen a bad boy--she had to experience one unfortunately.

I've had enough of bad boys and girls forever & ever. Unreliable, imposing, grabby, catty: danger.

29,000 users watching porn every second. Pea brains in the making and our country's wrecked hon'

The lunatic mob is drunkenness without wine. The goal is absolutely power in abrupt stages, aye.

Looks/status/connections/achievements are subject to flux/come and go: it's NOT who you know.

SOLUTION TO INNER EMPTINESS

The only way to end inner emptiness is to replace ego and the false self with love and goodness.

The narcissist can't replace inner emptiness because ego is all he knows and can't let go of.

The narcissist's worth, value and significance is in direct proportion to your LACK of these.

Constantly putting your down [with success] while elevating himself implies inner emptiness.

You thought he'd be happy for you, thrilled at your great success but no, he's mad and ghosting you.

It feels so curious, this dynamic of rejection of success but it's basic so expect it and nothing less.

You're not gonna get an introspective analysis from a narcissist, he has NO tools/escapes this.

TOAD TO PRINCE

If you get big he gets small, that's the way it is for a narcissist though the only remedy is love.

It's actually a drive to take from you to give them evidence they're a somebody, unbelievably.

They're always evaluating who's better. They're impressed by the outers but are wreckers

Even if they spurred your growth they're not happy since it triggers their original inferiority complex.

IF YOU'RE UP HE'S DOWN: HOMEOSTASIS

Inner emptiness is really triggered by another's success but yet they can't replace it with goodness.

They're constantly in a competitive one-up/one-down mode with discussion and you can't open em.

Inner emptiness is always triggered by one's success and yet they can't replace it with goodness.

Narcissism is a very frustrating and painful place to be since there's always more competitors see.

You try and try to get an introspective conversation but he simply doesn't have the tool set darlin'.

Inner emptiness can't adore you like you want. It's gotta be two wholes coming together love.

The closer he gets to his core the more he panics, runs away and now you won't see him any more.

FIND THE NONDESCRIPT MAN

Most narcissists are handsome and flashy so them being this way breaks many hearts surely.

TOAD TO PRINCE

Compare this to a nondescript man who is nevertheless **WHOLE** inside and can love and provide!

Give up the flashy one and dress up the guy who can really relate, introspect, love and discuss.

You've tried forever to get inside him but you'll never get a real conversation cuz the tools are missing.

It's not this heartbreaker you're in love with, it's the **NEXT** one now that you're a wise chick.

The constant one-upping is all due to evaluation: I got an A and you got an F kind of situation.

DON'T TELL EM ABOUT SUCCESS

It's a helluva thing when you run to a loved one about your success and they just reject you sis.

High, low, better, good: this drives them heavily going back to being a bully in the neighborhood.

They can evaluate self highly by having someone lower around and that's where you're handy.

They'll collect evidence of your mistakes and use em when they need to support their case.

You may dream of marital bliss but it's just a fantasy honey and I hope now you'll see this clearly.

These are psychological dynamics of those who've been traumatized and you can't change it, aye.

Take these words to heart, I've known/loved many narcissists. It's a dark path of painful thickets.

He can't get past his ego-protection and armor to love you dearly. It takes two whole people honey.

TOAD TO PRINCE

Find a man who doesn't care about looks or other's perceptions of him: a self-contained man.

With a narcissist everything is compensatory. You go up, he ghosts/goes down in a cycle of doom.

SUCCESS BRINGS REJECTION

He asked for a divorce on the same day she got her Ph.D. Homeostasis--it happens unfortunately.

Their personal sense of well-being is so externally based they've gotta have "clout" and "power" sis.

If he's seeing prostitutes on the side God'll ghost him [let him] so you can be a nice man's bride.

This is why they tend to gravitate to attitudes that imply aggression, one upmanship, domination.

A woman thinks: that's my tough guy, he'll protect and provide but no, it was just narcissism, aye.

Aggression makes em dominant so warning: watch out. There's no winning even by failing after all.

In entertainment they're drawn to themes of power, dominance, tyranny and often violence.

Inmates are running the asylum in universities. Kids throwing tantrums but teachers are complicit see.

THE COMPARATIVE MINDSET

With a comparative mindset the narc overlooks the necessity of self-reflective thinking.

They're so busy elevating themselves and comparing they never question why they do things.

TOAD TO PRINCE

It's impossible to delve into plus & minus because they're so busy with their evaluative status.

We rid inner emptiness by emptying ourselves of the false self and ego, but that's impossible.

The biggest mal-adaptation of the wife of the alcoholic is to get drunk herself then she's the target.

WOMEN BRINGING DOWN THEIR HOUSE

To women seeking greener pastures: Take stock of where you're at and who enabled that.

Who built the barbeque, who put in ten cat doors--start adding it all up and then rethink it girl.

Women seeking greener pastures ruin their lives, bringing their own house down, aye!

System Turn: When high he seemed to really love her but when she fell he became a monster.

That's not loyalty thru thick and thin. Looks, status, connections are subject to change thru time.

Women seeking to screw the guy thru the divorce court business are now being disappointed.

Her girlfriends advise asking $1500 a month for life then the judge gives her $250 instead, aye.

Mine was a story of the prodigal son. I was high then went way low, actually a learning mission.

LIFE CAN BE HIGH OR LOW/UP TO YOU

I'll never forget my past low points, it was so horrible it's a fright to even think about any of this.

TOAD TO PRINCE

God will punish sin that's the lesson there. New life will be wonderful compared to the old scares.

Women: don't even show desperation to your girlfriends cuz they're sharks too and will move in.

You gotta be strong now, a queen. Quit showing your feelings/don't rule with your emotions see.

Because people are cruel and ageist remarks aren't cool so you deal with & manage the despicable.

For me it's not about making a name for myself but getting my point across to forestall a mess.

A broken queen will be toyed with by the world of perverted male society: it's not pretty.

A woman unaware of who she is abused by the world: a queen pimped by a clown on the corner.

A queen expected to degrade herself like that? Get away from me buddy & never come back!

How does it happen a woman with everything is manipulated by a man shallow and empty?

It's a funny thing but clown knows right away you're not a queen so swoops right in as bad king.

How something like this can happen is a fascinating question and it has to do with feminism.

Lettered but still insecure and deliciously delighted that she can make him dependent on her.

THE QUEEN PRESENCE

Her presence is defined by her view of self ok--about what she will and will NOT tolerate.

TOAD TO PRINCE

A true queen views herself in a way where certain things are not negotiable--and most is intolerable.

If he's mentally ill but thinks he's well--and if he happens to have a youtube channel?

When a queen's established in her own heart what's nonnegotiable her actions are automatic.

A queen won't tolerate insecurities in herself for example, she conquered that before now.

She's made up in her mind: I'm not tolerating that [e.g. insecurities] and that's the queen archetype.

A queen knows whatever she tolerates the world takes advantage. She's learned, had enough of this.

The world is full of em: clowns, tramps, fools. You better learn not to tolerate: disgust is cool.

God said we wouldn't be condemned so she boldly says **NO** without fear of the mockings of men.

The height of your walls reflects your level of disgust and that's a good thing your highness.

A queen expected to degrade herself like that? Go to hell buddy along with your whole dam generation.

TO QUEENS IT'S INTOLERABLE

A queen won't tolerate insecurity cuz it comes from sin or not looking out for things enough/often.

Don't tolerate or you'll be taken advantage of. Don't sin or shame will hand control over to chumps.

A nonnegotiable is a standard you are incapable of falling beneath. You can't go lower see.

TOAD TO PRINCE

A queen is fundamentally incapable of falling beneath that standard. Only if she becomes a drunkard.

For if she fell beneath in behavior it would break her soul and divorce her from self: disaster.

NONNEGOTIABLE STANDARDS: CAN'T GO LOWER

Breaching a nonnegotiable breaks her soul and loses self. I've experienced this and it was hell.

When one is young and unself-aware there are things he will tolerate and the world pushes back ok.

I have standards for myself from years of trial and error—feeling consequences of doing whatever.

You're not gonna see me living different from what I say cuz they're nonnegotiables of the intolerables.

We all have a mindset. The mindset of fools is worldly but with royalty it's preset without debate see.

Our mindset precedes the world, the world does not impose itself on it. Those who do are twits.

YOUR MINDSET VS. THE WORLD

Our mindset precedes world, the world does not impose itself on it. Those who allow that are twits.

The higher you are the more disgusted and degree of disgust reflects your height: the king's might.

Why many queens won't drink: it lowers standards. They cope with other sins less dangerous.

A queen drinks and has a brazen affair in a blackout sir. She can't tolerate that unqueenlike behavior.

The world is constantly seeking to conquer [establish the mindset of] the queen and it's mean.

TOAD TO PRINCE

The tidal wave force of the world on the mindset means she must be ready, firm, set in hers, bad.
Everyone seeks to influence the queen and she's impervious and ready for that: go away/get!

When unwise I allowed so many things that were intolerable to me--I went against ME see.

Things that grit my nerves I allowed to be a good hostess or whatever. I was a weasel/unclever.

You must be able to say NO, go home, I won't have this here, I can't tolerate it: a test to pass for sure.

CHANGE THE QUEEN'S MIND!

They resent you queen and wanna tell you things that'll swing you to their side but you don't blink.

If she doesn't have her mind set the world will subvert her into a lesser version of self.

A lesser version of self will never match success. You gotta be full throttle of confidence.

Liberals always accuse you of what they're doing. They accuse YOU of what they DO.

The world is constantly pressuring you to turn it down a notch, to suppress highness = a mess.

If you don't see yourself as royalty but just a sex object its blatantly female slave conditioning, yuk!

The world tries to force us into a perverted sex mold but a queen won't degrade herself/look old.

The narcissist is a chameleon: one minute morphing to fit thru a keyhole, next a raving monster/bold.

TOAD TO PRINCE

Tho' she never had a dad to pour into her self-esteem she works on her soul with God as a team.

If you're born to do something that's all you wanna do. It's so intense you don't even eat/sleep too.

Of course she doesn't date--why be subjected to perverted expectations? To date makes her irate.

NOW HAVE CONFIDENCE & CERTAINTY

Having pre-established her matrix when she enters the world it's with confidence and certainty.

The queen is no toy to be played with nor easily manipulated and you'd better know it.

She's not so naive and gullible to be malleable in the hands of a perverted society of cuckolds.

Pomegranate juice and bread. Salad. Smoothie with fruit, dates, banana and cacao nibs in it.

She knows who she is, she knows her worth and demands her price due to nonnegotiables.

These people are not thieves, they have simply gone mad with hunger. Warsaw ghetto 1942

Confidential. Strictly secret. That's the atmosphere and I'm thru with it/have matured beyond it.

Few mention toxic siblings but if they gang up on one the results can be criminal and sadistic.

Sibling abuse was never what I wanted but as my whole reality I may as well write all about it.

By putting focus on envious jealous siblings it settled all doubts, the puzzle filled in and I was free.

TOAD TO PRINCE

JEALOUSY, ENVY, BITTERNESS

It's not just basic sibling rivalry it's malicious and sadistic sibling abuse. Dana Arcuri

Sibling rivalry is a common term but few realize its usually about hostility from jealousy.

Two separate things: sibling rivalry and toxic abuse. Rivalry's common but don't confuse the two.

It's when it crosses a line that it becomes abuse leading to PTSD. It can be physical or emotional see.

Millions are awakening to the fact it wasn't just rivalry it was sibling abuse and very malicious too.

They're steeped in a feeling of powerlessness that they can't control you and that is their distress.

They're angry they can't control the good and positive energy coming thru your accomplishments.

Siblings are caught in a comparison trap. If they didn't compare there wouldn't be this envy crap.

Jealousy is rooted in evil motives. These underlying deep intentions are demonic, better believe it.

ENVY IS HATRED

Envy is at its root hatred and bitterness and it's deep. Anyone with advantage is their target see.

Jealousy and envy are evil and sinful. God hates these, they are not of the Lord and it's biblical.

Enviers show passive-aggressive behaviors of gaslighting, gossiping or inciting wars.

TOAD TO PRINCE

The jealous will tell lies about you, spread rumors and triangulate all your relationships too.

Take something that's a teeny tiny truth and twist it into full blown fabrication about: YOU.

Mom's friends kept telling me my sisters were very jealous of me and that's why so mean.

I ignored these warnings but during gatherings I'd feel cues, triggers, secrecies, conspiracies.

DON'T IGNORE THE SIGNS

Out of peace-at-any-price I kept pushing it aside but reached a point where I had to call it out.

The core root is jealousy, hatred, bitterness and envy. Think of that when yearning for family.

Combined with these nefarious feelings are the INTENT FOR HARM. Realize this. Caution: alarm.

They'll do anything to devalue or shut you up--yes, the very people with whom you grew up.

We should be into our own thing not compare ourselves to others, we can even be happy for them.

SCAPEGOATS ARE SENSITIVE EMPATHS

To all super sensitive empaths: Keep peace with those stealing our peace is not a healthy boundary.

Scapegoat will lay low for a season then awaken, realize what happened then face the HATE.

Hatred is a sin and evil. The destruction that follows is a malignant cancer totally taking over.

TOAD TO PRINCE

The hatred is deep and evil and will sweep back as they reap the consequences, soul killed.

They will reap what they sow from the malignant cancer in them of hate and abuse against you.

With toxic siblings its constant backstabbing and rumors. Stealing, missing things, mobbings.

The youngest in the toxic broken family becomes easy prey to their instincts to block or soul slay.

Nothing new, jealous siblings from beginning of time and they often choose the youngest, it was I.

SYRUPY SWEET TO YOUR FACE

Syrupy sweet to your face then speaking horrible, hateful and vicious lies about you the Ace.

Always saying she was my friend but secretly wishing harm upon me, my life or possessions.

A malignant cancer, jealousy leads to revenge. They get vengeful, vindictively causing agitation.

They are going to punish you because they hate you and are jealous of you. You're a star? POOH

There's something so unique about you they'll stab you in the back at every opportunity too.

Parents who don't resolve family quarrels early will see far more dysfunction later believe me.

MALIGNANT CANCER GROWS WITH AGE

It accelerates thru life til it's a bomb ready to blow up = disease, divorce, getting locked up.

TOAD TO PRINCE

At this point you can't resolve something that's gone on your whole life. You go no-contact.

At this point you're fed up: DONE with siblings who are envious and deviously secretive in hatred.

We feel they are unaccountable for their hatred and jealousy but not true/the karma is cruel.

Hatred & jealousy are evil sins--reap what they've sown. Tho' they flourish they will be mowed down.

The inevitable longterm consequences to hatred and jealousy we can often see in the elderly.

Look at a whoremonger now in his sixties--his sins show on his rotting face the same as with hate.

We can't stop them or change them. All we can is release the toxicity by severing all relations.

It's been a lifetime and life's too short. By the time you realize the full extent of this, you're out.

It's like a contagious disease and we can't be a part of it. That means every one, relocate if it fits.

TRIANGULATION-STRANGULATION

Budding into your relationships: Triangulation, a deceitful form of manipulation to abuse.

Narcissistic triangulation involves a third person or more and it's always to control life like a rudder.

Narcissistic triangulation is also used by toxic abusers like sociopaths and psychopaths.

Psychopaths/sociopaths and women! Women are great abusers of triangulation, it's how they win.

TOAD TO PRINCE

Triangulation is their way of disrespecting us and our boundaries, of going behind so to speak.

Whenever triangulation occurs there are no healthy boundaries, you're being invaded mentally.

Triangulation is shame-based. The message is: you are not enough and our whole problem is YOU.

The narcissist is NOT about facts and truth. They are cunning & sly in their intentions for you.

HALF TRUTHS AND WEB OF LIES

A clever narcissist will take a half truth and web a spin of lies about the black sheep--was that you?

These tactics could be by a narcissist or simply someone who's toxic--very unhealthy to be with.

The goal is to destroy relationships, the tool is triangulation, the end: marriages break down.

ME: It's not so much a Creative Act as it is a journey--one that takes up your entire life see.

GOD PULLS PLUG ON BEAUTY: PRINCE TO TOAD

One way to self-love is to enforce the boundaries you've laid out. Do it NOW then you'll love yourself.

Here I thought you were so cool but it turns out you're nothing but another dam fool, a zero: pooh.

They start out a green tree that we're jealous of then God pulls the plug on beauty and they're ugliness.

First God gives em up to their evil desires then they're dead--thrown on the ash heap of non-history.

TOAD TO PRINCE

We're told not to envy the flourishing tree that later is like the grass mowed down/removed from history.

I'm so bad ass fabulous I'm not gonna go there anymore to be pushed in the mud by a man I should deplore.

God my Father was pissed off how he was abusing me so he pulled the plug on his beauty--what an ugly!

I'm Number One or forget it. Not gonna compete with this mediocrity so now you're the one who lost it.

They come from good stock in LOOKS but degenerate quickly thru sin. Old men sinner/has-beens.

I'm so glad to be outa your grasp. You can't get me now, I've seen the light and have gone WAY past it.

You're a sneaky one. The comeback kid, always with a greater shit shot to keep me down under a lid.

I'm gonna disable you now. If I don't go there it's as if you don't exist and I'm no longer so bored: wow!

SIN BRINGS UGLIFICATION

When God pulls the plug on beauty it's a sudden thing, a depedestalization: all light is gone, old/ugly.

God restores youth as the eagle so it's not irrevocable when you fall but really hard to revert back, y'all.

You can see this uglification from sin in old sex sinners: such a muddy aura prevails in their later years.

He's been with a thousand women, ten thousand! He brags about it but now at 60 REALLY shows it.

After bragging about all his sex sinning to get approval of youth, he looks old and ugly and they eschew.

TOAD TO PRINCE

But the fact he can get **THAT** old and ugly, not sure he can revert back. It would be astonishing in fact.

The flesh is weak and you really see it in old sex sinners. There's no logic to it: hanging/withering losers.

GOD RESTORES YOUTH AS THE EAGLE

Of course if he were to **REPENT** today and become a saint, God could restore his beauty and anoint.

A woman who cheats on her husband or tears down her house will lose her beauty or look gross.

Despite shiny make-up she has no shine due to a muddy aura around sinners increasing thru time.

There's two systems--living or dying--and the sinner goes into death no matter how many face-lifts.

ALL sin brings compensation in the present. These compensatory behaviors are neurosis/signs of it.

Making sexual comments to get the approval of the crowd only to get very ugly before them, cowed.

I got your number now. You failed, got ugly and so I've overcome my enemy in this, the greatest story.

VISAGE: SINS SHOUTED FROM ROOFTOPS

Start standing up for yourself. Heck, they'll take as much as you let them, miserable grifters all of em.

My last nasty image of you is engraved in my mind now and that's where it's gonna stay--hurray!

For I am **FABULOUS** and you're not gonna treat me like this cuz I see where it originates in my past.

Why are old sex sinners so ugly? Cuz they're filled with spirits of all those women + all their men: seedy!

Take a look, just take a look. See what happens to men like that after years of living as a liar and crook.

It all shows in their visage: that's the science of Physiognomy, sins shouted from rooftops.

BUT AS FOR YOU...
Real success resembles Tsunami: A giant wave of frenetic activity just after nothing, zero, silence, apathy.

GOD SAID <u>WHEN</u> YOU FAST [NOT IF]

Fast after noon--clear the system for deep sleep to ensue. Ignore advice or take raisins, a few.

Know how to eat. When hungry eat fruit as you start your soup then fast all day, that's the scoop.

The paradox of the Old Lady Diet is you end up looking like a young girl as you open up to the world.

It's like Ramadan Fasting without the evening meal: The breakfast-only plan for the saints is ideal.

Due to a kink in her colon she ate once a day only. Any more putrefied, leaving her constipated and lonely.

Since I've stopped dieting, whole new worlds have opened up: healthy thin, just from no sup.

TOAD TO PRINCE

Bulimia is an ugly green demon from hell. it's affecting millions of love-starved women in a shell.

You need animal foods--plants have anti-nutrients, tell millennials. Carnivores eat fruit and leaves but proportions vary/it's ok to eat cheese.

DAILY FASTARIANISM FOR SUPERIOR MEN

Congenial body: There are times I can't see your charms but it all comes back when you're in my arms.

Feel the gentleness of your new congenial body free of disease/smells good and sure to please.

You can be cute with the strength of a fleet, just don't eat. This is Daily Fasting 18 hours/don't cheat.

If the skin is filled with crud, the sun will age it/cause cancer. But if detoxed, for beauty it's your answer.

Don't eat after noon or before a.m. 6. Can you do this, can you get healthy/prevent getting sick?

Skin, hair and eye color is determined genetically but cannot be seen until transfusion of the bloodstream.

The curative powers of daily fasting are superior to the vitamin deficiencies you fear.

How weird that the food enjoyed for breakfast will kill you at night--just skip dinner and it's all right.

You gotta do the work, outside agents won't work. But fortunately the work is fun/each day gets better hon'

Elimination is anti-gravity--that's age--so start eliminating and become a sage

TOAD TO PRINCE

My solution for sleep apnea: Don't eat past noon. Haven't choked since and love fasting in the afternoons!
Who wants to have their face wrapped around their head? Forget face lifts and just eat right instead.

Go for nutrient density (energy/beauty) not empty calories (tired/bloated/ugly).

We need optimal nutrition to offset early diet abuses, diseases or empty calories: malnutrition.

KINGS NEED NUTRIENTS

More nutrition per calorie means satiety: not ever being hungry.

Nutrient density writes your looks, empty calories create uglies and kooks.

Food Science is all about proportions, pyramids, ratios and main players.

No need to fight over diet, just eat right and show it then a contagion of enlightenment (they'll know it).

72% of our food is processed with a low antioxidant/micronutrient load and that's why Americans resemble toads.

Actresses in 1945 had 19" waists and pretty. Not just real food but no chemtrails (make us ratty and stubby).

Maximum longevity occurs when BMI is below 23. All else is superfluity. Feed the hungry: tell the truth.

ROYALTY GETS PRETTY

During WWII the men were handsome and the women pretty. Now it's the bears or the dirty ol' bitty.

Youth-glorifyers insult post-thirty. Despite accomplishments it's a trick, dirty. Solution: fast (get pretty).

It's easy to put various things into the smoothie like an apothecary then sip it all morning merrily.

TOAD TO PRINCE

Some people can eat hundreds of carbs a day, some only zero: we're all different, that's what I know.

All animals select right amount of protein/fat as long as they're eating the right foods, get that.

No elaborate recipes! Keep it simple then paradise. No more concoctions! Yuk, think about it. Just what it is, perfect.

Kicked out of ketosis means weight gain and cravings. Breakfast-only plan is satiety without gaining.

If food causes problems why not just eat once a day? Things will be swinging—you'll love life this way.

FAST FOR BREAKTHROUGHS

You've been at a standstill. Nothing ever happens, bitter pill. How to break the block: fast until.

If you're on the right diet day or night you're high as a kite but when you sleep it's deliciously deep.

Though I discovered it as a teen, it took decades to realize the power of daily fasting--joy everlasting.

By tapping into the ultimate food source—your own fat of course—you'll eat less and move more.

Your body knows how to melt fat, just give it the tools and eat like a cat.

Einstein proved less is more: most creative energy comes in least mass and that's why I fast.

PSYCH DRUGS ARE THE DREGS

The night you made an ass of yourself publicly, all from anti-depressants you took decades before—ole.

TOAD TO PRINCE

We've given up on medicine and don't know whether to be happy or sad but glad to rely on God our Dad.
You may have gotten violent, vituperative, argumentative, demonic--that's from psych drugs, honest.

Drugged: Having blocked impulse control, any notion normally forgotten takes hold/society scolds.

Any horrible act from blocked impulse control is explained, it wasn't you it was psych drugs of the day.

Two weeks of anti-d's and three years later had unexplained rages against husband, delayed effects.

Chemicals make you insane, morally too. It's about impulse control and inhibitions--and they knew.

LOOK GOOD, GET POWER

From Life Sux to Fasting Rox. News should be on every block: never felt this good around the clock.

Learn to love fasting. It's the magic key in all races/religions but staying thin/high are my reasons.

It all depends on your food window. 5-8 hours is best then 16-19 hours fast.

Who are they to tell us what to eat? But I let em do it (30 bananas a day) because I was weak.

Some are genetically encoded to eat 90% fat. Others need veggies and fruits, can you believe that?

Wives killing their husbands through wrong fat-protein-carb ratios: What does he need, does she know?

What you should eat: genetic predispositions vs. allergens, and first foods eaten in adaptation.

I can have one digestive burn a day but if I dare have two--acid, bubbles, misery: it's hell to pay.

TOAD TO PRINCE

I loved the taste but what it did to my body was a disgrace.
Music/fasting was what the doctor ordered after all this: years of Obama or people distress.

Everything but music tracks into the left brain: movies and news take me outa the groove, they drain.

SHORT FASTS ARE A BLAST

72 hour water fast produces stem cells and regenerates immune system.

Intermittent fasting is total rejuvenation tho' it's a short duration.

Fasting doesn't just eat cancer tumors it eats old scars internally, divinely.

Intermittent fasting: You have to be strong to do it and it makes you strong so you can [have fun/intuit].

I am done dieting, it did me in cuz I couldn't use intuition.

As long as you know them all there's nothing wrong with moving between diets. In fact it's the highest.

I've done em all: fruitarian, fat, lowcarb, highcarb, raw, cooked starch, paleo-- good if ALL of em you know.

The high-fat diet is not for everybody. Restrain to veggies and starches if you want high-fiber misery.

I love to see the body transform through austerity, taking charge, being positive and looking ahead.

You can wait for ketosis if you want to but I'm doing it the old fashioned way: don't eat and get slim.

You can try fruit for breakfast and protein for lunch, to see if the early sugar will be too much.

Banned by diet Nazis again. Who cares it confirms my points which are rare.

TOAD TO PRINCE

Maybe the reason we keep switching back and forth is cuz we're supposed to?

Reversal diet: Stay thin through instinct alone not diet dogma cuz we're all different and only you know.

My mother stopped eating--it's a stage and had to do with age.

Be real excited about getting the fat out, you know your perception is widening so shout joy out loud!

STRONG BODY, OVERCOMING MIND

Forget calories and just fast after fat. Plants are low calorie but high ANTI-NUTRIENT.

Do it the old fashioned way: counting calories? Never bother with these if it's just fruit and cheese.

Eat fat, go into ketosis. That's the theory but don't eat again or results could be disastrous.

I'm moderate carb (fruits) and high fat—also known as the Most Delicious and Natural Diet of Reversals.

If lowcarb works for you, have at it. But I grew a bulge and the scales divulged that: mono-dieting, dump it.

They developed deficiencies: fruitarians only eating fruit/greens and dumping all fats to be skinny.

It goes back to Arnold Ehret, the first book I read. Fruits, greens and everything else sits like lead.

For some time I won't go back to starch, I don't crave feeling stuffed and blocked up like that.

The meaty/fatty ("delicious") foods of kings is called Higher Quality (HQ) but Daniel glowed by refusing em.

There are times I want fat/nothing else, there are times just fruit works for elves but the fast is for ketosis.

TOAD TO PRINCE

High fat/starch diet results in abdominal rolls for some but fruit dissolves encumbrance of the tum.

Had to ditch keto Kate and butter Bob. Their way may work for them but it made me look odd.

Did I make a diet mistake? No, experimentation is vital, can't just listen to what you're told.

You can keep your lowcarb fatty meats/dairy. Made me crazy if just that but it's all solved with berries.

DAILY FASTING IS FUN

Eat meat, "wait for ketosis" which never happens. Add fruit and fast instead, you'll be fans.

The little ladies of the fifty's stayed tiny cuz they knew how to do it intuitively.

Melt it down through fruit breakfast, push it down with protein lunch, fly high skipping dinner (just a hunch).

Reverse between heavy and light--carnivore with fruitarian: use it like a rudder day and night.

Been interested in diet since age ten so of course it was all experimentation, bringing health vacillation.

If reversal dieting is the most efficient then it's not vacillation or indecision, it's the best hon'.

Banana-berry smoothie and the fat pockets are dissolving, I fast all day and can feel it curing.

So far, so good: Organic breakfast then fast--fat is releasing/feel so sparkly and no acid or dizzy.

If you don't feel like eating anyway why not just live on smoothies, cherries, grapes and berries.

TOAD TO PRINCE

A peaches and cream complexion comes from fasting after breakfast not from food, don't forget that.

Reversal Dieting: Feel stuffed with butter, look forward to future when fruit makes it better, rid of the fetter.

Feel like I have a couch in my gut after my experiment with high-fiber diets but the fast takes it all out.

When patterns are broken new worlds emerge. Stop hating them and abundance comes in/you can splurge.

GET CLEAR, HAVE CHEER

An event occurs and the disease symptoms roll out. It's genetic as symptoms respond to life stress markers.

A stress level is reached and the genetically predisposed disease erupts—fast to breakout.

I will no longer diet to my detriment ever again. Just make it organic but the rest is defilement, it is sin.

Some keto dieters wait and pray for ketosis as the scales continue to rise--it's not working, guys.

Sip smoothie all day, dissolve fat pockets. Persevere then shoot up like a rocket/you can do it.

No matter how much you advanced the other view, the new you knows it's not true just a detour [whew].

In the Old Lady Diet we enjoy music and move all around. Through music we're big in a small town.

RID ORTHOREXIA: NO DIETING

The only sure cure for orthorexia is not living on any diet from that point on-- it's a wonderful life, hon'.

TOAD TO PRINCE

I love the chocolate, a natural magnesium laxative and it makes me feel so good and very active.

Bulimia is a bad memory/brings remorse. She didn't know how food made us ugly and sick so she tried to fix it.

Nutrient density bring satiety after the smoothie so I can fast all day to the next--I love living this way.

As you fast you'll leave the realm of eating. It's another world above the fray/you won't be cheating.

Eat, then fast. It's like a lift-off or rocket launcher and you won't be hungry just having a blast.

Guess that's why some say all food is poison. But I think I got around it all by the daily fasting lesson.

They run out of pot then take antidepressants or succumb to beer and it's so much worse my dear.

Marijuana is an herb as-is. Other drugs are designed, manufactured, adulterated—crap for masses.

For some THC takes away the pain, going to that part of the brain.

One digestive burn: Incredible, wonderful, energizing, good morning. Two: hell on earth, bubbles, burning.

RELEASE FROM DIETING MADE ME HIGH

Of all the great releases in life, release form diet made me the highest.

Digestion requires 85% of your available energy so one burn I can do but more is impossible.

The more intelligent are not obese while the less are, devoid of necessary impulse control of stars.

The RX insert says you're gonna have dizziness, nausea, chronic flatulence and maybe death.

TOAD TO PRINCE

Fat is what brings up the calories so if you're fruit only--save eating crates of it--it's low-cal/on the money.

What, you'd rather have a bean burrito filled with cheese than your mate's love becuz you please?

People get old, they die and no one ever remembers them after that so why worry if you're fat?

Make note of your bad looks after apple turnover from Arby's. Now never deviate again or stay wanna-bes

Anorexia Psychosa is a mental illness from starvation hormones--careful how you judge a bag of bones.

I believe healing is all diet not outside agents--too easy, forget it. That's my two cents, take it/leave it.

The food is unnatural = ugly, bloated, sick and dead. God's nutrition (from the ground) is the only way to be fed.

It's health equals nutrient density/calorie. Empty calories make you bloated, sick, old, dim, angry and rickety.

It's easy to get fat on a diet not designed for humans/irrelevant if you fry it.

LOOK GOOD/BE STRONG

A processed-food eater with normal weight is sick in some way. Fuhrman

If they live long enough all who eat this food will develop heart disease or cancer as revealed by the numbers.

Sorry for my insanity under the influence of the wrong food, truly.

We find health not through gluttarianism but eating the right food: nutritarianism.

Reason for nutritarianism (nutrient density): cancer prevention and longevity--compensation, early life correction.

TOAD TO PRINCE

Sign of being out of ketosis is weight gain--symptom of disease. If you're fat get into ketosis, please.

Man is fat from wrong macronutrient ratios

There are two results of eating past noon: Heartburning or choking when you should be sleeping.

Fast and they want you to eat--to push you off your pedestal of beauty with the strength of a fleet.

KILLING CHEMICALS

Our world is thick with chemicals. They make the sensitives sick but since most are impervious, they're skeptical.

Other people's homes are like gas chambers cuz they're naive about things like everyday cleaners.

If a Universal Reactor there's no way to make plans--just be ready to get away from stimuli which offends.

Chemical sensitivity: I can be so well only to get so sick then get so well: change seats, recovery is quick.

All you can do is lower total load: get purer, cleaner, simpler to enable handling poisons everywhere.

Chemical sensitivity demands you manage people too. It's an energy budget and you can't afford the shrew.

Fortunates who are impervious to chemicals doubt those who aren't, calling them malingers, stupid, not smart.

MULTIPLE CHEMICAL SENSITIVITY HELL

MCS solution: Live on smoothies/salads/soups and stay home (no commotion).

You're not "in the country" as long as neighbors burn trash. It's carcinogenic, we're sick, expect backlash.

TOAD TO PRINCE

Flu Shots are packed with crap. Doctors always ask but you must refuse to maintain your life and health.

Got sick, got well just moving from the stimulus. Mom thought I was faking sick to skip school I guess.

With Multiple Chemical Sensitivity how can I make plans with you? I can't know how I'll feel: old/blue or new.

Many think you're trying to get sympathy. Dealing with these misjudgments is part of the malady.

For those with chemical sensitivity, life's a balancing act. To lower the load you take a warm bath/have a nap.

Social gatherings making me sickest. It's cumulative--total load goes way up whether poor or the richest.

JUST STAY HOME

You learn to just stay home: Where you feel good, everything's controlled, no hearts of wood.

I make home life so fascinating there is never a reason to leave. There is nothing out there but to deceive.

Success: Make a nice home for a man so he'll never want to leave, then he makes money--just believe.

As we get older life becomes fuller not lesser cuza more memories to see the present through: spectacular.

In old age we shoot to the mostess as the temporal lobe bursts open to reveal eternity: So how is it a tragedy?

I just wanna stay home. No where else, no matter how nice, get off my case, the answer is no cuz I'm the ace.

Don't like social obligations cuz that's what they are--obligations. Just wanna stay home with my creations!

TOAD TO PRINCE

Nothing out there interests me—no-thing. My own home is where it's at so please stop bugging me.

BODY SWEET

Genetic codes are unique. Some can take 200 carbs daily, some zero and even a meat diet only.

A boring diet gives you an exciting life, satisfied.

My husband healed/became his True Self through my food: my selections and preparations were proved.

I've seen too many fat families where one got thin to think it's not eating habits learned from family/friends.

Families teach kids to talk and to eat. That's why they're fat--not genetics cuz through food we unplug from genes.

Gabbing and gorging go together: Be a faster and stop habitual and idle chatter.

Food God made = perfect features/smooth skin. Food man made = you're distorted and pasty, man.

GENTILIZE YOUR SPIRIT

Personal carb-fat-protein ratio is genetically encoded and until you select that your health is demoted.

Our internal genetic program will automatically choose the right foods (% of protein/fat) as will a dog or cat.

Elaborate recipes bypass our ability to stop or choose right: do not eat these concoctions tonight.

Dieting is not about will power but freedom from food cravings instantly, every day and hour = personal power.

When dogma trumps genetic code we live in a shell: Like vegans eating just fruit and mad as hell.

TOAD TO PRINCE

Change the ratio and perfect the source later--get to it fool. Get it all at Walmart if you have to.

Getting into ketosis is more important than what you eat so soar through the sky, no reason to cheat.

The distance between you and health is hours. Transit Time as food goes through for the fast = new powers.

CURE THYSELF

When eating right and you're full, stop eating and body digests gut rolls--it's autophagy: perfecting it all.

Just change your macronutrient ratio: do it. That's more important than the source of it.

Be a model: No matter what your age, you are able. Do it for your pet projects like the elderly or animals.

If fit the older man looks better than the young--the opposite to all you've been told (bunk).

The most important thing about food is satiety power, not "nutrients" but it's the same, me thinks.

Many vegans dream of meat. That's their genetic code begging to cheat.

You know your protein-fat-carb ratio: lit's what you crave but you're dissuaded by those in the know.

Gabbing and gorging go together: Be a faster and stop idle chatter.

GET QUICK AND SLICK

Your genetic code is the best of your ancestral past and if it says 90% fat, it is best to go with that!

The ability to choose the right foods (protein/carb/fat) comes when we eat right, just like that.

TOAD TO PRINCE

Without all those meals I'm so much happier. Low fecal bulk is so much prettier and the gut is flat, sir.

Big guts are fecal cuz the diet is fickle. Stop sayin fat is genetic cuz it'll go out and not in a dribble.

You can be young again! All you gotta do is pray, fast and repent of compulsive food sins today.

LOOK GOOD WHEN OLD

You may need the lion diet if it suits your temperament. You get many things done every hour and minute.

Love handles and saddle bags are from the wrong food for you. The way to slimness is to watch what you chew.

Have pride through diet. It's not just not-frying-it but also the self-discipline it takes and they can't deny it!

Fast: spend the day with God. Then the True Self emerges and it's futuristic and mod--they'll be awed.

They're trying to kill us. Chemtrails overhead: they target individuals but want us all dead.

IBS IS FROM CHEMTRAILS

IBS is a result of chemtrails. Take yogurt with fruit cuz digestion and the good bacteria fails.

Deliberately giving us respiratory illness like COPD--we're on inhalers or nebulizers from this tragedy.

Trump disappoints to the degree he does nothing about chemtrails making us old and sickly.

Salt and chemicals in the air: geo-engineering not in text books, unfair.

You may not notice it, you accept a low level of life and carsick feeling. Even vertigo—reeling.

TOAD TO PRINCE

Deliberately trying to kill us and extremely interconnected, a web of chemical weaponry and constant.

Barium is the problem. They plaster us with it, bedridden. Carcinogens, crop-killin, memory gone.

Chemtrails raise total load on immunity so we're getting sick with just a small stimuli, continuously.

No more beautiful skies just cloud cover, haze but mostly pollutants.

Controlling the weather is a dangerous weapon due to far-ranging implications like water/food ration.

Can't go to churches even the back pew due to chemical sensitivities, thank you.

Can't go to gatherings due to chemical sensitivities must stay at HOME with air cleaners you see.

Detox with pineapple while you pump up good bacteria with the yogurt and it's a marvel for sure.

Gut aches: One Old Lady Diet was raisins, nuts, pineapple and yogurt. Not cuz she wanted it but all else hurt.

GET OUT THE LEAD AND TURN HEADS

The tolerant tell women to put up with their weight. You mean they should just accept mean fate?

Ugly weight centers in the mid region. To prove it try on some hip huggers and see the bulges which are legion.

People should not be gaseous. If constipated it's due to food eaten: change the diet and it's beaten.

It's the same with your dogs: if they are flatulent you gave em the food, so correct this before God.

TOAD TO PRINCE

Genetic type is our biochemical makeup determining the best ratio of fats-proteins-carbs, that I know.

Bulimia is an ugly green demon so stop it or be seen as vermin.

We require different ratios of carb-protein-fat. Some want mostly veg, some need fat like the cat.

When reversing between fruit and fat a unique trigger evokes sudden weight loss. Trigger loss = you're boss.

Some require minimal animal, huge amounts of veg--but that would spell disaster on me/the rest.

A bad habit is something you do in cycles. You swear off but then it comes around to hit you.

I stay thin and never exercise. I just work, run up/down stairs and avoid false ties.

Cook: gotta do it just to fill the tank so start a routine of soups, stews/whatever you do then get to work.

THIN, PROPRIOCEPTIVE, SECLUDED

Cancer victims can't eat but they can drink: Put raw milk, banana, fruits in blender/get in the pink.

In the past, cancer victims refrained from raw milk but now they see it's a cure, with skin like silk.

If you can't eat, drink smoothies to give yourself superior elements.

Eating is a youth thing (you want it all) but later it's hardly anything (the lovely fasting call).

Anti-depressants cause rage/depression sometimes decades later after cessation, who needs em.

Old Lady Diet: Smoothies, Soups, Stews, Seed chips

TOAD TO PRINCE

Different body type = different temperament. Ectomorphy (thin) is more proprioceptive/secluded.

This banana-berry-kale smoothie is nutrient dense but that's not true with the bread or rice.

Cancer cure: raw milk-fruit smoothie daily.

Raw milk/fruit smoothie crucial but cure is from eliminating the harmful.

What we want is nutrient density so make your curative salads right in your greenhouse and enjoy.

Eating like a bird: seed crackers after smoothie.

Low digestion, high nutrient density = seed cracker after smoothie.

To hell with low fat crowd. Fat is what makes life delicious and satisfying but they're the most loud.

Adding fat to diet I felt so much better. No more hunger pains or having to eat again/love a little butter.

You can tell by looking at someone they've got worldly bloat and it's from the food, you know it.

If I didn't use a little butter on veggies I'd be hungry and an avo doesn't cut it and it's not as tasty.

Without fat in diet I'm hungry all the time. Maybe it's genetic but this lowfat thing seems a crime.

Few modern diet dogmas would put sweet fruit with lacto (dairy) but to me it's perfect with *energy*.

HUMANE DAIRY AND GRASS FED COWS

Make sure it's a humane dairy with grass fed cows. Raw milk cures cancer along with the *grapecure*.

TOAD TO PRINCE

You're suposed to be lowcarb or highcarb but refuse these designations and eat dense once a day son.

I like my fruit/yogurt smoothie in morning then a veggie with butter/garlic sauce--French approach rocks.

Lacto-Fruit: FFF is fruit, fat and daily fasting.

Not too much starch either, it hits the gut like a brick. Just produce with a little fat = gut stays flat.

Delicious cheese, cream and butter sauces on my veggies are so I'll eat it. Otherwise, I'm not interested.

Rice, noodles, potatoes, bread—it may be vegan and even satiate but to me it's a gut full of nails.

After my French lunch not hungry till breakfast. Just Skip Dinner because satiety will surely last.

Anytime a sauce has butter, salt and pepper, garlic and simmered WOW of course I'll eat and enjoy it.

I blend up in the morning, lacto-fruitarian is essential. Now be ready for anything even evil.

Don't eat past noon. Man up, give body a rest, fast and be blessed as truths are revealed of the best.

The idea of eating a big meal at night seems foreign to me--uncomfortable and impossible to sleep.

KRAZY KOLLEGE KIDS WRONG DIET

Krazy Kollege Kids are mal-adapting to the wrong diet. As liberals it's some kind of false diet dogma.

Eat fruits and meats, store nuts, seeds, cheese and use honey to make candies.

TOAD TO PRINCE

The way the Krazy Kollege Kids look is a simple case of wrong diet. Yuk: bloat, acne and lopsidedness.

If you wanna live on rice/bread go ahead but it lost logic to me no matter what I used as a spread.

Lowcarb and no fruit? Yuk three times that's impossible to compute but fruit and fat makes you cute.

No amount of micros can fix bad macros (fat, protein, carb ratio)--it's carbs for those in the know.

Starch eaters thin but a fat eater (seeds, nuts, avocado, olive oil, cacao) isn't fat with daily fasting.

BE PRODUCTIVE: SIT AND THINK

It's ok to sit and think as you look off to space--that's most productive other than puttering all day.

When you eat once daily, stop worrying about macros and just eat what you want to lose it all.

SRI's magnify weaknesses. So if one is insecure he plunges into bloated immaturity or bad friends.

It's not fat vs. carbs--it's both, in one meal.

Remember word: "essentiality". Keep only the essential (the quintessential) and you'll be successful.

We're meant to live at high speed until the moment we die--not decline, become obsolete, wither, cry.

If fats go acid--burning in the esophagus--are they truly good for us? Cacao does it too: yuk!

Man can adapt to living on fat but starches have sustained the human race thru time, that's a fact.

CREAMY LACTOFRUITARIAN SMOOTHIES

TOAD TO PRINCE

Fruit/yogurt smoothie, tacos, fast 24 hours: High as a kite doing it daily and feeling powerful.

The more people the more chemicals. I gotta say I just wanna get away to solitude and be a marvel.

I think 99 times and find nothing. I stop thinking, swim in silence, and truth comes to me. Einstein

When true reality blasts open you may cry for a night but then a new dawn makes everything bright.

The more I find myself the more people I lose. It should bring relief to know it's a process not you.

REPRESSED EMOTIONS & FOOD

How I cleaned up diet/ returned to childhood normal: Meat and water.

Repressed emotions bring false positivity like seeing humor in tragedy or losing touch completely.

Chocolate doesn't make you look like that and if it does, never eat it--it's BAD.

People eat to avoid facing feelings/reality. So by not-eating they face it, reintegrate and get happy.

FFF: Fruit-Fat-Fasting is Fruit/dairy with 18 hours fasting daily. It's lacto-fruitarian fastarianism.

When momma's home it's food and cooking, snacks and hugging, music and eternity, loving!

In exact proportion to how I cleaned up my diet, the pain stopped.

In exact proportion to how I cleaned up my diet, immunity came back.

In exact proportion to how I cleaned up my diet I became a cute chick.

TOAD TO PRINCE

How to get to success: Take the day off.

One acre plots ain't out in the country. Need 20 acres minimum or it's chemicals/unhealthy.

OUT IN THE COUNTRY BUT STILL SICKLY
Need Protein Honey

"Out in the country" doesn't mean never sick. One-acre plots (PEOPLE) and they burn, spray, gossip.

One acre plots means men always building things with particle board/glue and burning trash too.

Country neighborhood just as toxic as the city if they're burning trash or listening to officious ol' bitties.

Trash burning: Beautiful country life--can't breathe. Gorgeous views--sick as hell wanna leave.

Feels like old London with dark murky air. I'm in the country but neighbors burn trash/don't care.

They'll burn you out and rob you blind.

Ten more pounds--to be cancer-free you gotta be skinny if you have the propensity.

Ride the wave with holy spirit ease (humming), or if in sin be bumped outa grace (nothing, unbecoming).

No matter how bad just hang on/soon you'll turn a corner. Life tests then rewards non-drunkards.

I don't believe this: "Fat paralyzes insulin/increases insulin needs". John MacDougal

Wheat-bellies aren't sneaking in fat cuz it's the starchivores that end up like that: high fiber is a rat.

TOAD TO PRINCE

Have butter on bread and if just one meal it may be ok. But for me, fat and starch built bumps (dismay).

You're middle aged and acting like that? Don't you see what's happening as we're poisoned/made fat?

BUMP IN THE BELT CUZ NO FRUIT

Why do the lowcarb gurus all have a bump at the belt? Not a beach ball belly but definitely not svelte.

You say you're sooo fit but there a belly bump. The abs and tummy must be FLAT to be fit, bud.

Cancer radiation builds beach ball bellies. Bloated men you see have often had it/not an anomaly.

The wealthy meat and dairy industry loves the lowcarb theory. They pump up these fat gurus heartily.

People wanna hear good news about bad habits. Meat and butter's good but not ever the fruit with it.

How can political vegans make their point to other people by looking so terrible? Anger triggers devil.

VIOLENT VEGANS

Attacked by vegans as phony cuz thanksgiving he takes a bite of turkey.

Just by looking good, being well-informed person and getting in their face—do it. John MacDougal

People love to hear good news on bad habits--like eat all the butter you want, no need to resist.

They're pushing lowcarb for the money: lose weight, be unhealthy.

Much of it was due to poor diet but also the things I went thru early before I knew it and I blew it.

TOAD TO PRINCE

Vegan militants: I hate the tyranny of the movement and the ridicule if you break code even one bit.

NATURAL HYGIENE USED TO BE KIND

Natural hygiene (fruits/veggies) used to be a kind, gentle thing. But now it's like SJW's/it's worrying me.

It's not about your being superior cuz you eat a certain way--that's like the social justice thing, ok?

Separating us from land is medical tyranny cuz they're the ones who'll make the disease-money.

They don't want us farming/kids aren't taught. They want us in city ghettos living on GMO's we bought.

One is nearest to God's heart in a garden, and it's a natural and fascinating thing to children.

The more sugar, the less insulin resistance and it cures diabetes (opposite to what they tell us)?

Dr. MacDougal looks so good and look what he's up against: the meat and dairy industry hoods.

Sugar makes insulin work better and cures diabetics--opposite to what we been told by non-legit.

They put down sugar so we'll switch to dairy/meat instead--pushing lowcarb/confirmed by med.

MODERATION OR MUKBANGS?

He's great cuz he binges in mukbangs?

Things work better with tomato cheese for lunch.

You get the trial--pass it/God gives you ALL.

TOAD TO PRINCE

You can't lambaste them for it, you can only withdraw and build back up. Take a music vaca.

When God convicts it's easier to quit.

Let em party: wine, dine, dance. Soon they'll be a mess: breech lines, get fat, take a bad chance.

Torturous slow death and shortens life by 20-30 years: Yah let's give it to em, there's nothing to fear.

Even tho' inserts say drugs will kill ya, they don't care they're gonna make your take vaccines, ya hear?

We're gonna poison you/sexualize your kids. We're gonna put you on drugs with a 33% increase in death.

Omnivorous bodies can adapt to various diets. Like shiny yogis living on milk and fruit, believe it.

"Don't mix fruit with milk, berries with acid fruit, don't put bananas in it too"-- forget restrictive rules.

OLD LADY DIETS

Raw milk, yogurt and lotsa fruit in a smoothie. If not for that some couldn't eat, like the old ladies.

Europe has raw milk machines throughout. Not drinks with aspartame carcinogens, throw em out.

Old lady lived on a huge smoothie of lotsa fruit/yogurt sipped thru the day and happily lived that way.

He drank wine from morning till night--his wife mal-adapted by becoming a sorry, psychotic blight.

They drive you crazy with their food combining rules. Learn what works and do it your way, fools.

TOAD TO PRINCE

Life's too short for this orthorexic crap. Enjoy your food, enjoy life and live it through your OWN MAP.

Grace Jones lives on 4 dozen oysters a day: beautiful at 70, great example of living your own way.

Don't tell me not to eat bananas with pineapple. Cram rules: be like a baby choosing what is natural.

If you wanna drink pond scum (green drinks) go ahead--I like sweet fruit with full-bodied yogurt instead.

A genius breaks all rules. But first he's gotta learn em and the integration makes life so cool.

OLD LADY DIET IS ABOUT ATTITUDE

The healer of the future must show the effects of the cure in himself. Arnold Ehret

Digestion raises total load, using 85% of energy: the breakfast-only plan relieves chemical allergy

Age 130: one daily meal of yogurt, fruit, bread, honey, tomato, cheese. As an obligate carnivore I eat meat.

Female genius is rare cuz they're killed off early from drugs, suicide or incapacity to deal with snide.

Even tho' past abusers are dead the mental illness from their intrusions go on 'til God takes over instead.

"Sh*t happens" said the street philosopher. So true--now go on ahead and stay happy and sober.

It's in there/must be dealt with: the primal scream. Solution: new friends, smoothies with fruit/cream.

The primal scream from past abuse by the obtuse drove me to love James Brown/yelling thru the roof!

TOAD TO PRINCE

Tho' the culprits are dead still mental illness remains cuz it's stored in the body, pulling your chains.

HOLLYWOOD CAN'T EVEN IDENTIFY CORRUPTION

Hollywood stars have no capacity to identify corruption even when it's standing right over them.

You gotta bring it up and face it. It hurts, I know it, I've been thru it but you'll be a new person: fit.

Dr. MacDougal is great--too bad he has to ruin it by getting involved with phony global warming debate.

Childhood obesity is ten times higher than forty years ago. Ten times more fat kids from 1977? Wow

If you have chemical sensitivities (MCS) you must relax (aft naps).

Old Lady Diet: Meat is least allergenic but lacto-Fruitarian, smoothies and soups if you want it. DAILY fast.

Soups, smoothies, piece cheese or nuts: no more acid or torturous bloating fiber.

Why does the Old Lady Diet include tacos? Because it's the only delicious food she knows.

Mom stopped eating: no hunger save tacos cuz they're raw, delicious and no acid repeating.

What's the food you recall from childhood, teen years, early adult? Tacos, tacos, tacos that's all.

Rice noodles are great for disaster storage and we enjoy them with shrimp on Saturdays.

TASTE TRIP WHILE STAYING HIGH

The Old Lady Diet's about taste without energy being dragged down to the gut and fatigue ruts.

TOAD TO PRINCE

She developed an eating disorder adapting to sisters and jealous putdowns creating misery.

Eat something solid = acid. Smoothies and soups: happy, peaceful, placid.

They're so darn rulish about everything but this works and that's the only thing.

Just to get calories so we can get back to work, we blend 5 bananas with berries, raw nutbutters/dairy.

The barium in chemtrails is giving us IBS and other gut issues but a liquid diet unblocks the tissues.

Diet dogma vs. seers: Stop telling me not to eat food man has enjoyed for thousands of years.

I can't eat potatoes cuz I don't have a snout to dig deep into dirt? Spuds kept whole continents alive, jerk.

Man's always had division of labor: the butcher, baker, candlestick maker.

Decades of fruitarianism I looked pail, wasted, old, busted. Revert to meat and water and I came back, rested.

LACTOFRUITARIAN DELIGHT

The only way you can eat once a day is to collapse calories thru animal fat, ok?

The lady said "Lactofruitarian smoothie's keeps me alive with a few tortilla chips, that's it".

Reversal Dieting: When I get too spacy on my fruitmilk shake a steak brings me back.

It took me so much pain to get to that place of seeing the efficacy of protein and fasting/not eating.

Eating or drinking at a problem is so debasing but fasting at it is total ace-ing and so elevating.

TOAD TO PRINCE

Between IQ and fat the relation is inverse: The smarter you are the less likely to be obese.

SIMMER ALL DAY

Boil and simmer veggies/herbs/spices for a long time, put in blender, now enjoy the old lady diet.

Health is an achievement: I can breathe again. Try detoxing, dis-fattening or clearing the terrain.

Coffee and chocolate due to ACID BURN is now off-limits to this kid.

Brunch: delicious high fat lunch with leaves while looking at the view so pleasing.

For years no butter on my baked potato but now I know it's ok if eating once a day you know.

CARNIVORE DIET

Meat and water ten days, you'll slim right down. Eat it once a day if you're like me and want results full-blown.

I was mentally ill from the effects of SRI's (anti-depressants) for three decades after just two weeks.

Chemical sensitivity brings on fear of disorder: cerebrotonia so avoid messers and junksters.

Nice break: It's just easier to fast then to constantly be going into the kitchen to fix something ok.

The hunger pain is gone then you can just stay at your desk and work all day without stop ok?

UPDATES RECENT 2022

Like magic Joyce Meyers changed me last night. An anointed preacher cues the good fight.

TOAD TO PRINCE

I promised God I'd watch Joyce daily now. She's doing me so much good with similar history, wow.

The sorrow of Ukraine shows how thin the veil of civilization is and what we take for granted.

94% of Americans know Biden's behind the inflation not Russia or Ukraine. We're sick of his game.

The NBA is protecting China. They said bring any signs you want except Free Uyghurs or Hong Kong.

100 KAREN KELLOCK BOOKS

AFFINITY OR MISERY
AGELESS CORNUCOPIA
AMERICA AWAKE!
AMERICA'S DAFT ERA
ARTS OF PALEO FASTING
AUTOPHAGY ON CHEATERS
BACKSTABBING NEUROTICS
BETRAYAL TRAUMA
BOOMERS AND BROKENNESS
BOOT ON NECK
CHAMPION GUIDES
COMMIE NUTHOUSE
COMMIES
COMMUNIST SPIRIT
CONTAGION OF MADNESS
CONTAGIOUS MADNESS
CULTURE CLASH BASHED
DAFT LEFT
DAILY FASTARIAN
DAM RATS
DIVERSITY IS CRUELTY
E-RACE WHITE
EVIL FREAKS (Beyond Gross)
THE END OR A BEND?
FEMALE BULLIES AND FEMI-NAZIS
FEMALE CARNALITY
FEMALE DUMB DOWN
FEMALE POWER DRIVE
FEMINISM AND RUIN 1 & 2
FIX FOR MISFITS
FOOLS & TRAMPS
FREEDOM SPEAKING
FRENEMY ENABLER
FRENEMY LIAR
FRENEMY THIEF
FRENEMY TRAITOR
TRENEMY TYRANT
GENIUS IS HELD DOWN
GLOBALISLAM
GOD USES THE FLAWED
HAZE OF THE LATTER DAYS

KAREN KELLOCK PH.D.

M.S. Political Science, San Diego State. Ph.D. in Psychology, University of California Irvine. Postdoctoral: UCI School of Medicine, Dept. of Psychiatry [NIMH Grants]. Developed the Debris Theory of Disease, a theory of system pathology in 120 books and 22 textbooks for the general public. The theory has a general formula: All disease is obstruction, all recovery is elimination, all success is attraction. The three obstructions are people, habit and food. Remove obstruction and snap to your goals, waiting in the wings.